Pebble® Plus
Bilingüe/ Bilingual

RAMAS MILITARES/MILITARY BRANCHES

LA INFANTERÍA DE MARINA DE EE.UU. / THE U.S. MARINE CORPS

por/by Jennifer Reed

Editor Consultor/Consulting Editor: Dra. Gail Saunders-Smith

CAPSTONE PRESS
a capstone imprint

Pebble Plus is published by Capstone Press,
151 Good Counsel Drive, P.O. Box 669, Mankato, Minnesota 56002.
www.capstonepress.com

092009
005618CGS10

 Books published by Capstone Press are manufactured with paper
containing at least 10 percent post-consumer waste.

Library of Congress Cataloging-in-Publication Data
Reed, Jennifer, 1967–
　　[U.S. Marine Corps. Spanish & English]
　　La Infantería de Marina de EE.UU. / por Jennifer Reed = The U.S. Marine Corps /
by Jennifer Reed.
　　p. cm. — (Pebble plus bilingüe/bilingual. Ramas militares/Military branches)
　　Includes index.
　　Summary: "Simple text and photographs describe the U.S. Marine Corps' purpose, jobs, machines, and
tools — in both English and Spanish" — Provided by publisher.
　　ISBN 978-1-4296-4603-1 (library binding)
　　1. United States. Marine Corps — Juvenile literature. I. Title. II. Title: U.S. Marine Corps. III. Series.
VE23.R4418 2010
359.9'60973 — dc22　　　　　　　　　　　　　　　　　　　　　　　　　　2009030384

Editorial Credits
Gillia Olson, editor; Strictly Spanish, translation services; Katy Kudela, bilingual editor; Renée T. Doyle,
　　designer; Jo Miller, photo researcher; Eric Manske, production specialist

Photo Credits
Capstone Press/Karon Dubke, 3
DVIC/CPL Robert R. Attebury, 17; LCPL Michael L. Haas, 11; MC2(SW/AW) Elizabeth Merriam, 13; PHAA
　　Shannon K. Garcia, 5
Getty Images Inc./David Greedy, 19; Science Faction/Ed Darack, 15
Photo by Ted Carlson/Fotodynamics, 9, 21
Shutterstock/Philip Lange, 1
U.S. Navy Photo by JO2 Zack Baddorf, 7; by PHAA Shannon Garcia, cover (front and back), 22

Artistic Effects
Shutterstock/iNNOCENt (white sand), cover (front and back), 1, 24
iStockphoto/James Kingman (metal in title), cover (front and back), 1

Note to Parents and Teachers

The Ramas militares/Military Branches set supports national science standards related to
science, technology, and society. This book describes and illustrates the U.S. Marine Corps
in both English and Spanish. The images support early readers in understanding the text.
The repetition of words and phrases helps early readers learn new words. This book also
introduces early readers to subject-specific vocabulary words, which are defined in the
Glossary section. Early readers may need assistance to read some words and to use the
Table of Contents, Glossary, Internet Sites, and Index sections of the book.

Table of Contents

Tabla de contenidos

What Is the Marine Corps?

The Marine Corps is a branch of the
United States Armed Forces. Marines are
often the first to fight for the country.

¿Qué es la Infantería de Marina?

La Infantería de Marina es una rama de
las Fuerzas Armadas de Estados Unidos.
Los marines a menudo son los primeros
en combatir por el país.

4

Marine Corps Jobs

Marines are trained to fight
anywhere. They fight on land,
at sea, or in the air.

Trabajos en la Infantería de Marina

Los marines están entrenados
para combatir en cualquier lugar.
Ellos combaten en tierra,
en el mar o en el aire.

Marine pilots fly airplanes and helicopters. They use F/A-18 airplanes to attack enemy targets.

Los marines pilotos vuelan aviones y helicópteros. Ellos usan los aviones F/A-18 para atacar objetivos enemigos.

Marines have other jobs too.

Mechanics fix machines.

Reporters write Marine news.

Los marines también tienen otros
trabajos. Los mecánicos arreglan
las máquinas. Los reporteros escriben
las noticias de la Infantería de Marina.

Machines and Tools

Marines use vehicles to get to their targets. The AAV can float on water and drive on land.

Herramientas y máquinas

Los marines usan vehículos para llegar a sus objetivos. El AAV puede flotar en el agua y puede ser manejado sobre tierra.

Big helicopters carry Marines
into battle. The Sea Knight
is a Marine helicopter.

Grandes helicópteros transportan
a los marines a las batallas.
El Sea Knight es un helicóptero
de la Infantería de Marina.

Marines also have weapons.

Each Marine carries an M-16 rifle.

Grenades and missiles blow up

enemy targets.

Los marines también tienen armas.

Cada marine lleva un rifle M-16.

Las granadas y los misiles hacen

explotar los objetivos enemigos.

Marines carry binoculars to
see faraway things. They use
binoculars and other tools to
find out about enemies.

Los marines llevan binoculares
para ver cosas que están lejos.
Ellos usan binoculares y otras
herramientas para informarse
sobre sus enemigos.

Keeping Us Safe

The brave Marines work together.

They are always ready to protect

the country.

Mantener nuestra seguridad

Los valientes marines trabajan

en conjunto. Ellos siempre están

listos para proteger al país.

Glossary

AAV — Assault Amphibian Vehicle; AAVs can float on water and travel on land.

Armed Forces — the whole military; the U.S. Armed Forces include the Army, Navy, Air Force, Marine Corps, and Coast Guard.

branch — a part of a larger group

grenade — a small weapon used to blow up a target

mechanic — a person who fixes machines

missile — a weapon that is fired at a target to blow it up

rifle — a weapon that can fire bullets very fast

target — an object at which to aim or shoot

vehicle — a machine that carries people and goods

Internet Sites

FactHound offers a safe, fun way to find Internet sites related to this book. All of the sites on FactHound have been researched by our staff.

Here's all you do:

Visit *www.facthound.com*

FactHound will fetch the best sites for you!

Glosario

el AAV — vehículo de asalto anfibio; los AAV pueden flotar en el agua y viajar por tierra.

las Fuerzas Armadas — todas las ramas militares; las Fuerzas Armadas de EE.UU. incluyen el Ejército, la Armada, la Fuerza Aérea, la Infantería de Marina y la Guardia Costera.

la granada — un arma pequeña que se usa para hacer explotar un objetivo

el mecánico — una persona que repara máquinas

el misil — un arma grande que se usa para hacer explotar un objetivo

el objetivo — un objeto al cual se apunta o se dispara

la rama — una parte de un grupo más grande

el rifle — un arma que puede disparar balas rápidamente

el vehículo — una máquina que transporta personas y suministros

Sitios de Internet

FactHound brinda una forma segura y divertida de encontrar sitios de Internet relacionados con este libro. Todos los sitios en FactHound han sido investigados por nuestro personal.

Esto es todo lo que tú necesitas hacer:

Visita *www.facthound.com*

¡FactHound buscará los mejores sitios para ti!

Index

Índice